CONFIGURING A BASE DYNAMICS AX 2012 TEST SYSTEM

BY MURRAY FIFE

ISBN: 1499678355

ISBN-13: 978-1499678352

Preface

What you need for this Blueprint

All the examples shown in this blueprint were done with the Microsoft Dynamics AX 2012 virtual machine image that was downloaded from the Microsoft CustomerSource or PartnerSource site. If you don't have your own installation of Microsoft Dynamics AX 2012, you can also use the images found on the Microsoft Learning Download Center. The following list of software from the virtual image was leveraged within this blueprint:

- Microsoft Dynamics AX 2012

Even though all the preceding software was used during the development and testing of the recipes in this book, they may also work on earlier versions of the software with minor tweaks and adjustments, and should also work on later versions without any changes.

Errata

Although we have taken every care to ensure the accuracy of our content, mistakes do happen. If you find a mistake in one of our books—maybe a mistake in the text or the code—we would be grateful if you would report this to us. By doing so, you can save other readers from frustration and help us improve subsequent versions of this book. If you find any errata, please report them by emailing murray@murrayfife.me.

Piracy

Piracy of copyright material on the Internet is an ongoing problem across all media. If you come across any illegal copies of our works, in any form, on the Internet, please provide us with the location address or website name immediately so that we can pursue a remedy.

Please contact us at murray@murrayfife.me with a link to the suspected pirated material.

We appreciate your help in protecting our authors, and our ability to bring you valuable content.

Questions

You can contact us at murray@murrayfife.me if you are having a problem with any aspect of the book, and we will do our best to address it.

Table Of Contents

INTRODUCTION

There is no better way to start learning Dynamics AX 2012 then to just dive in and start setting it up from a blank slate. As you start sculpting your system you are able to see how everything fits together and will also give you the muscle memory that will make you a ninja when it comes to using it in the future.

For traditional ERP systems, this is easier said than done because you need to first get the system installed, and then you don't know where to even start. Luckily with Azure Hosting, and the pre-built demonstration environments that Microsoft deliver through their Lifecycle services, firing up a new system to test in is a breeze, and once you have a sandbox to play in, creating a new partition that is clean and ready for you to start tinkering in is just as easy.

In the following book we will walk through the setup required to deploy a test system, and also configure a blank partition so that you can start learning Dynamics AX.

USING AZURE AND LIFECYCLE SEVICES TO HOST YOUR DYNAMICS AX TEST SYSTEM

Azure is a great place to host your Dynamics AX environment, because it means that you don't have to invest in any hardware, servers, or high powered computers to run the test system. If you play your cards right, it may not even cost you a cent...

To make this even easier, Lifecycle Services offers a Cloud Hosted Environment tool that will create a Dynamics AX environment for you that is hosted through the Azure services within a couple of minutes – give and take 30 for the machine to be deployed. This is a great way to create a test system without requiring any investment in hardware, or software.

Signing Up For An Azure Account

The first step in this process is to make sure that you have an Azure account with Microsoft.

Signing Up For An Azure Account

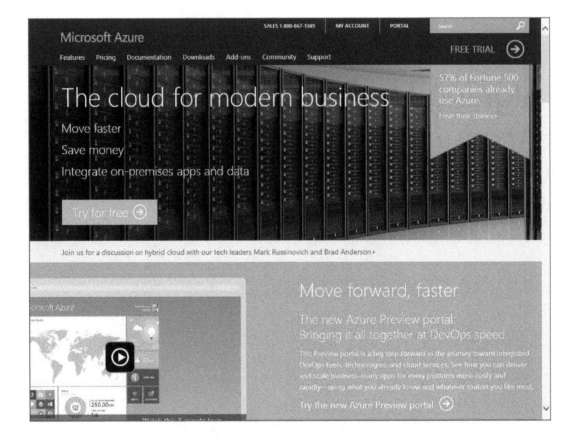

To do this just go to the Microsoft Azure site where you can sign up.

Signing Up For An Azure Account

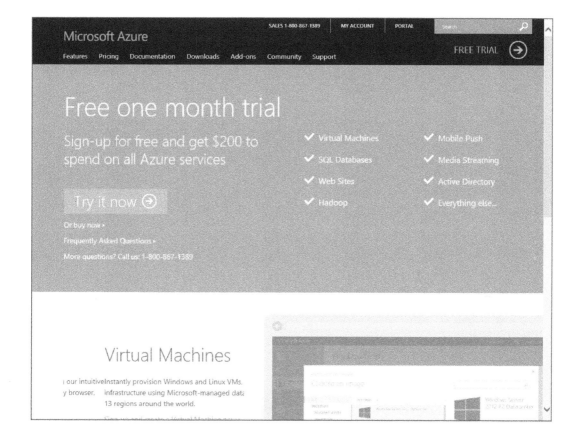

If you're lucky you may even be able to catch a promotion to test out the service.

Signing Up For An Azure Account

Also, if you have a MSDN account, then you may also get free credits towards your Azure account as well. This is what I use.

Once you have signed up, note down your **Subscription ID**.

Creating A Dynamics AX Instance On Azure Through Lifecycle Services

Once you have an Azure account, you can use Lifecycle Services to create a virtual test environment for you that is built off the standard demo system that Microsoft have built and populated with sample data.

Creating A Dynamics AX Instance On Azure Through Lifecycle Services

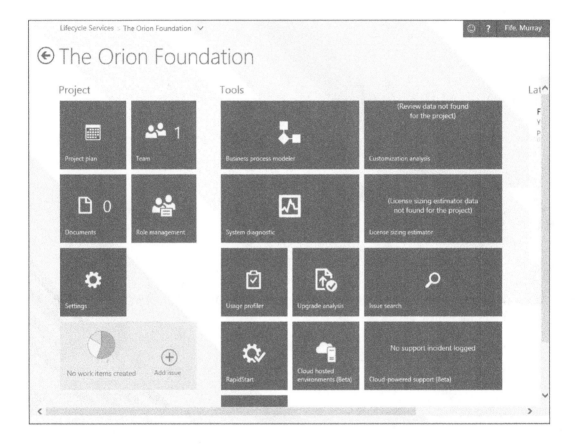

To do this, open up Lifecycle Services, and open up the project that you want to deploy the environment for. Then click on the **Cloud Hosted Environment** tile within the **Tools** group.

Creating A Dynamics AX Instance On Azure Through Lifecycle Services

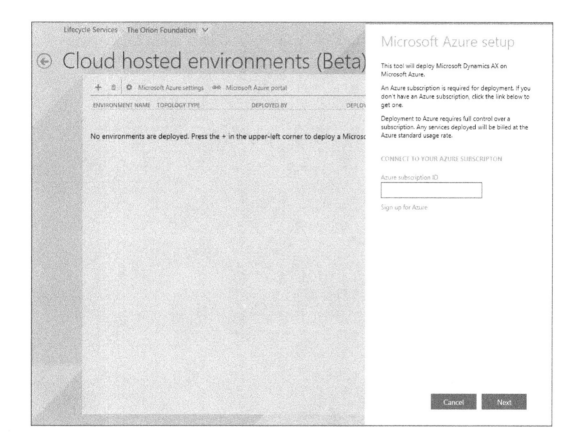

Lifecycle Services will then ask you to specify the Azure Subscription ID that you are using to host the virtual machine in.

Creating A Dynamics AX Instance On Azure Through Lifecycle Services

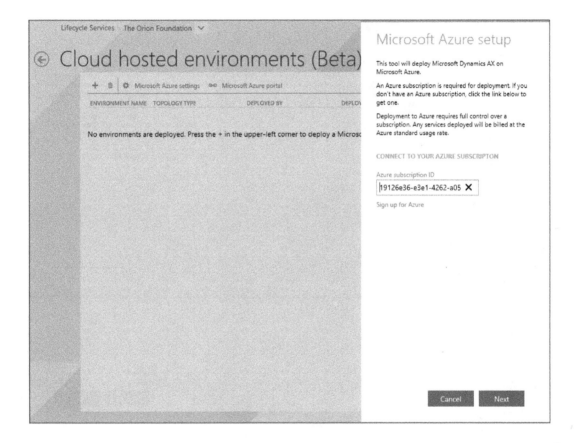

Return back to Lifecycle Services and paste in your **Azure Subscription ID** and click on the **Next** button.

Creating A Dynamics AX Instance On Azure Through Lifecycle Services

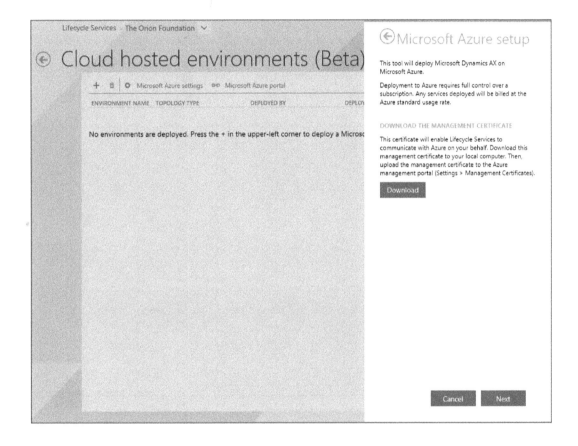

Then you will be asked to link Lifecycle Services with the Azure account. To do this, click the **Download** button to get your Management Certificate.

Creating A Dynamics AX Instance On Azure Through Lifecycle Services

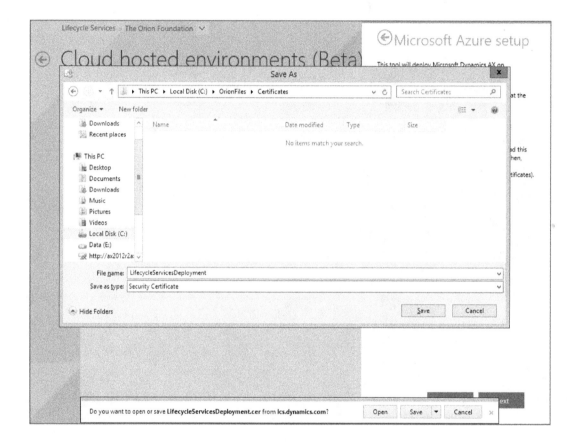

Then save the Certificate to your desktop.

Creating A Dynamics AX Instance On Azure Through Lifecycle Services

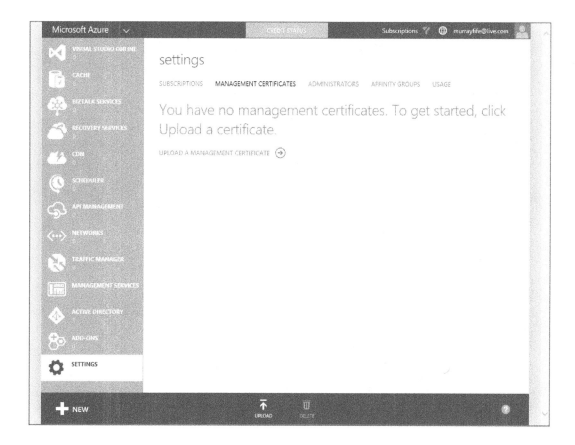

Return to Azure, and select the **Management Certificates** tab within the **Settings** group and then click on the **Upload** button in the bottom bar.

Creating A Dynamics AX Instance On Azure Through Lifecycle Services

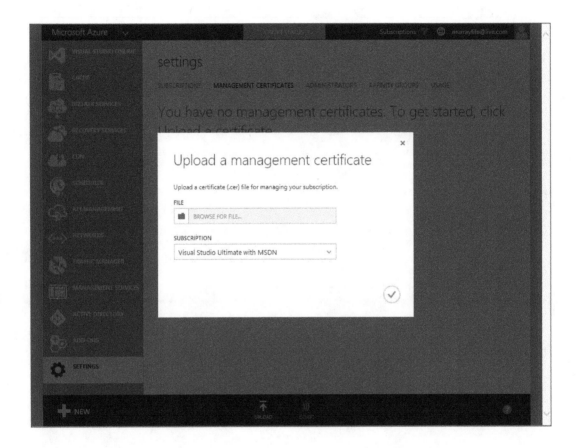

When the **Upload A Management Certificate** dialog is displayed, click on the **Browse For File** link.

Creating A Dynamics AX Instance On Azure Through Lifecycle Services

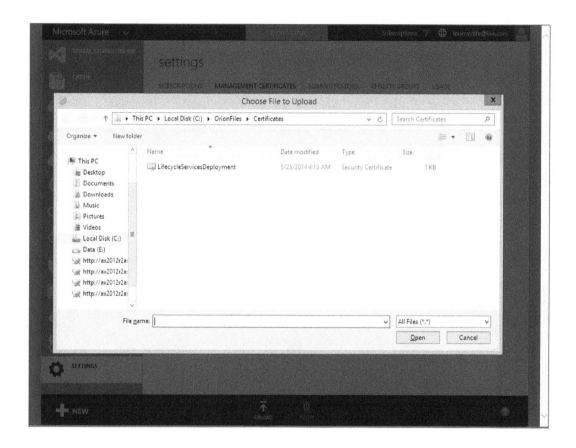

And then find the management certificate that you saved away and click the **Open** button.

Creating A Dynamics AX Instance On Azure Through Lifecycle Services

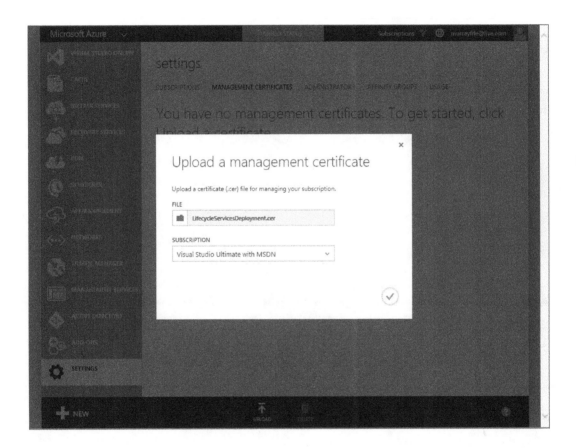

Then click the check box to upload the certificate.

Creating A Dynamics AX Instance On Azure Through Lifecycle Services

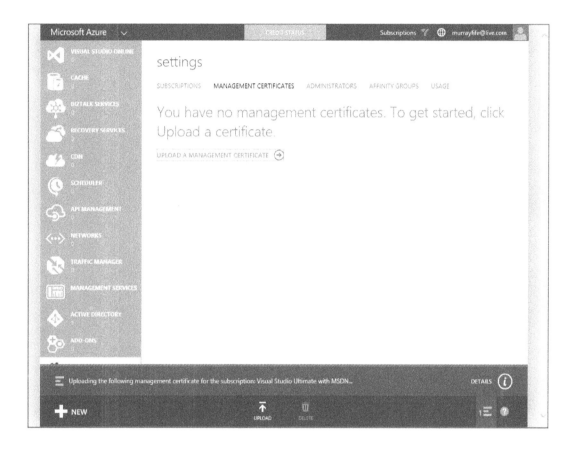

Now within Azure you should have a new **Management Certificate** record.

Creating A Dynamics AX Instance On Azure Through Lifecycle Services

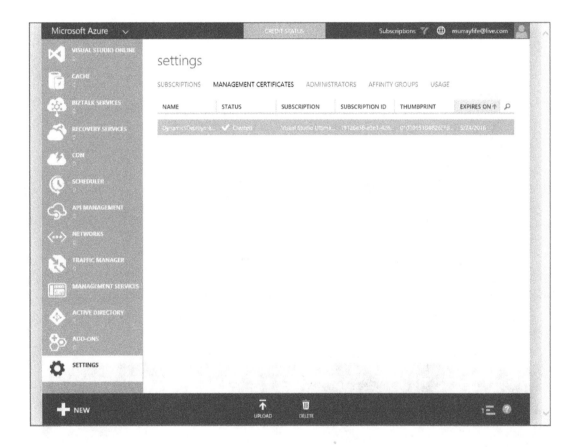

Note: it may take a minute for the certificate to upload.

Creating A Dynamics AX Instance On Azure Through Lifecycle Services

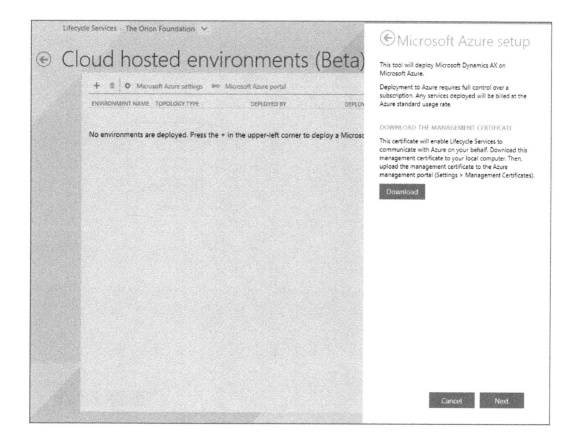

Now return to Lifecycle Services and click the **Next** button.

Creating A Dynamics AX Instance On Azure Through Lifecycle Services

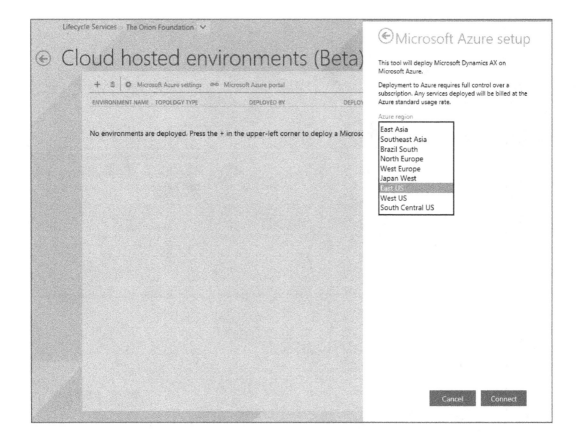

Specify your region, and then click the **Connect** button.

Creating A Dynamics AX Instance On Azure Through Lifecycle Services

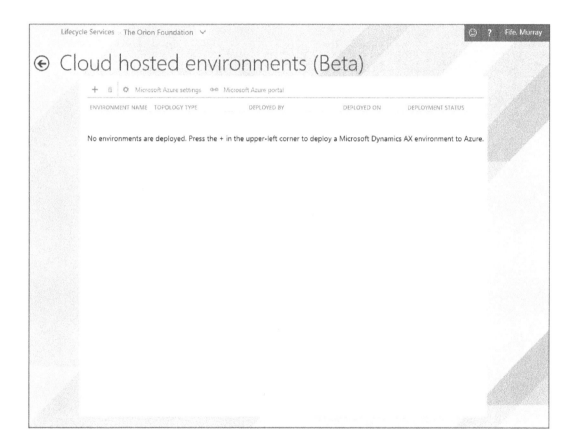

Now you will be able to access the **Cloud Hosted Environments** list form. To add a new demo server, click on the **+** icon in the top left of the form.

Creating A Dynamics AX Instance On Azure Through Lifecycle Services

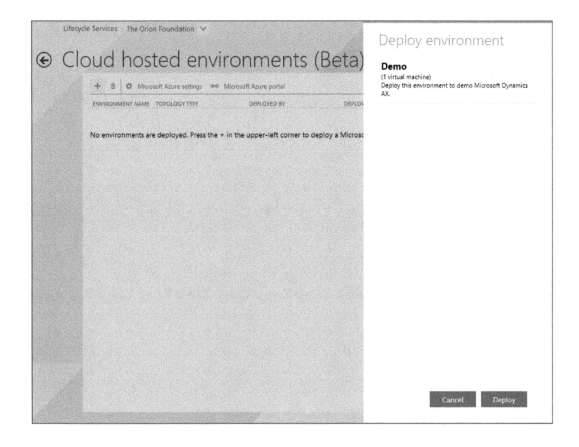

You will then be given a list of possible environments.

Creating A Dynamics AX Instance On Azure Through Lifecycle Services

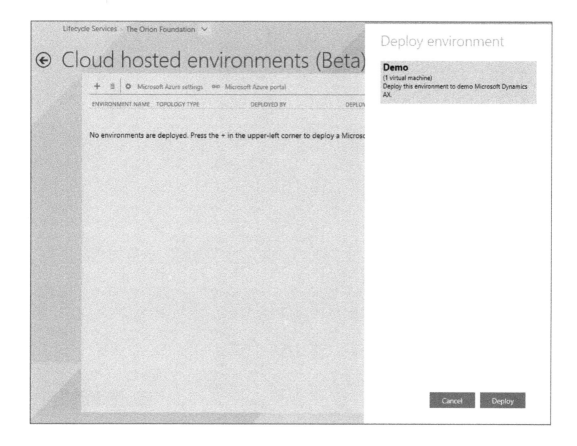

Select the version that you want to deploy and then click the **Deploy** button.

Creating A Dynamics AX Instance On Azure Through Lifecycle Services

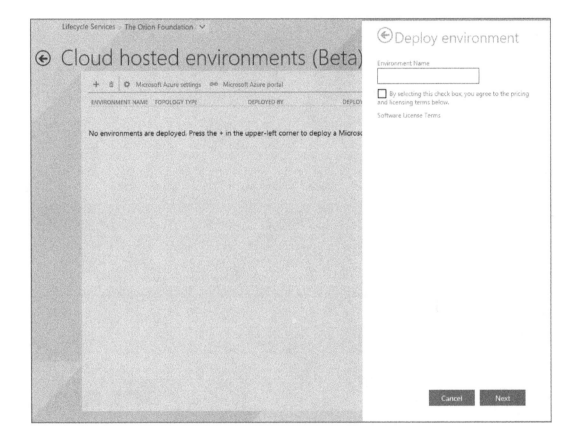

You will then be asked to set up your demo environment.

Creating A Dynamics AX Instance On Azure Through Lifecycle Services

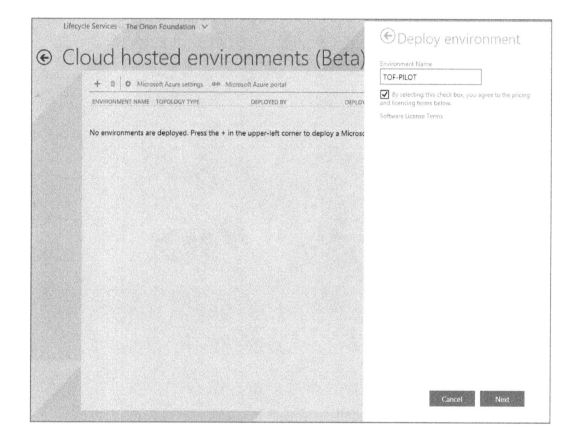

Give your environment a **Name**, check the mandatory agreement box, and then click the **Next** button.

Creating A Dynamics AX Instance On Azure Through Lifecycle Services

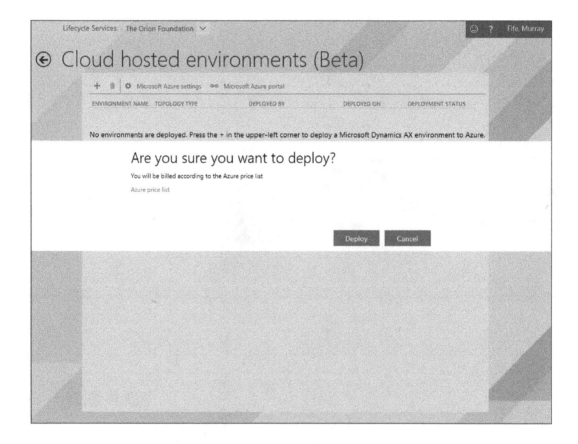

Finally, if you are sure that you want to do this, click the **Deploy** button.

Creating A Dynamics AX Instance On Azure Through Lifecycle Services

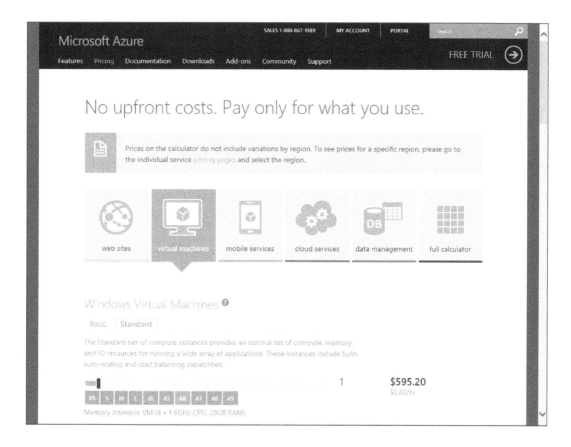

Disclaimer: If you run this particular version of the demo without turning it off then keep in mind that it will run you about $600 a month.

Creating A Dynamics AX Instance On Azure Through Lifecycle Services

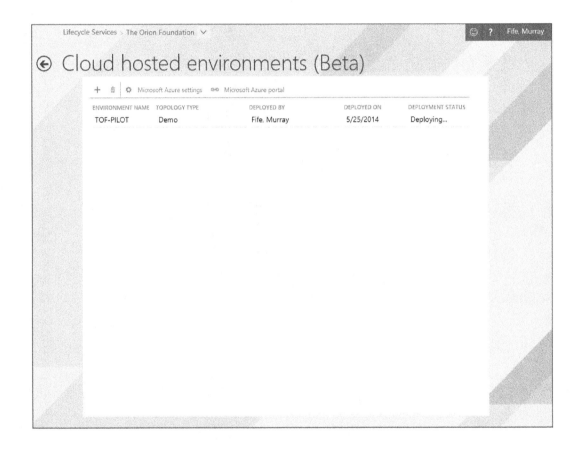

Now Azure needs to do a little bit of work to deploy the image. Now would be a good time to get a coffee – it will take 30 minutes or so.

Creating A Dynamics AX Instance On Azure Through Lifecycle Services

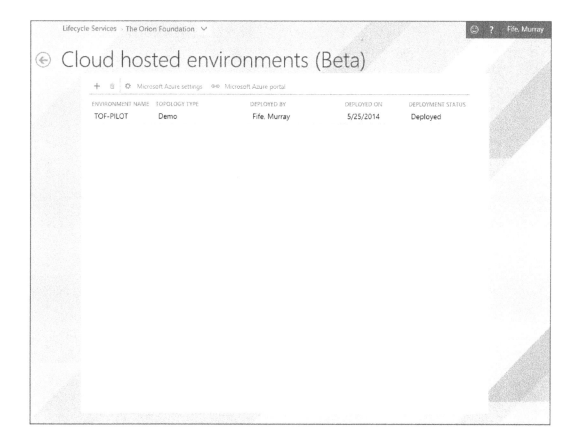

After a little bit, you will find that the image has been deployed.

Creating A Dynamics AX Instance On Azure Through Lifecycle Services

If you return to your Azure account you will notice that the server is now available. To access it just click on the **Connect** button in the footer of the form.

Creating A Dynamics AX Instance On Azure Through Lifecycle Services

And you will be able to log into the demo environment.

Creating A Dynamics AX Instance On Azure Through Lifecycle Services

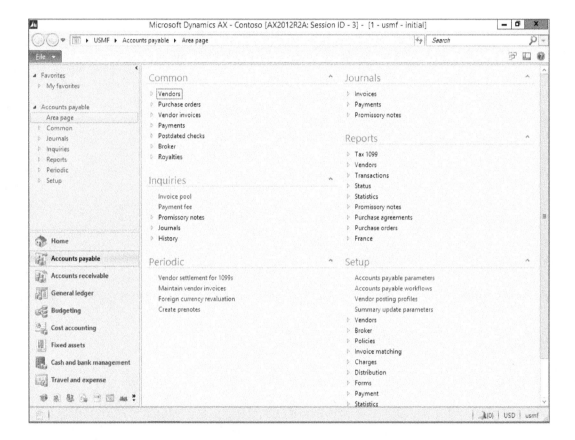

And Dynamics AX is already configured for you with the demo data.

That is super cool.

Creating A Dynamics AX Instance On Azure Through Lifecycle Services

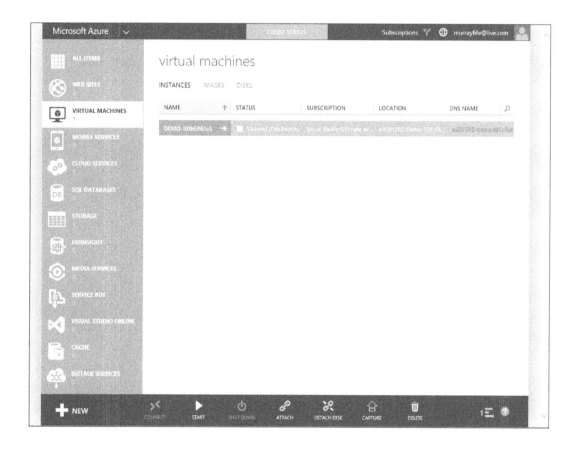

Tip: So that you don't get hit with a large bill at the end of the month, when you are not using the VM, just turn it off.

CREATING A NEW PARTION

There is no better way to start setting up Dynamics AX then from a blank slate, and the easiest way to create a blank slate within Dynamics AX if to create a new **Partition**. Partitions are great because they allow you to create a completely new version of Dynamics AX within an existing installation but all of the information is completely stand alone.

In the following worked example we will walk through the configuration of a new partition so that you can build and use one to configure and learn Dynamics AX through.

Creating A New Partition

The first step in the process if to create a new **Partition** for your system.

Creating A New Partition

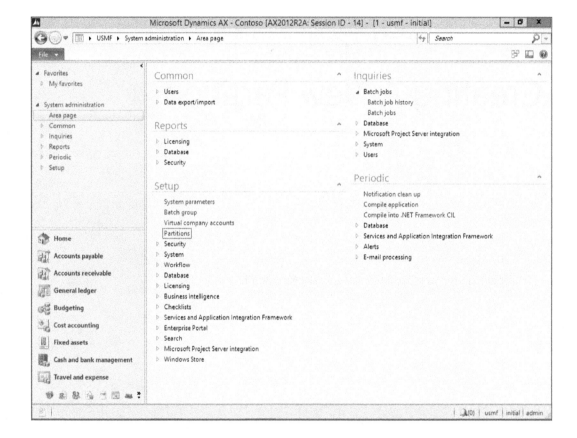

To do this, click on the **Partitions** link within the **Setup** group of the **System Administration** page.

Creating A New Partition

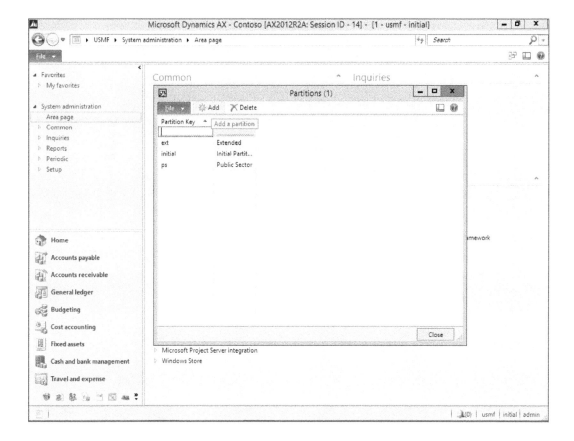

When the **Partitions** form is displayed, click on the **New** button within the menu bar to create a new **Partition** record.

Creating A New Partition

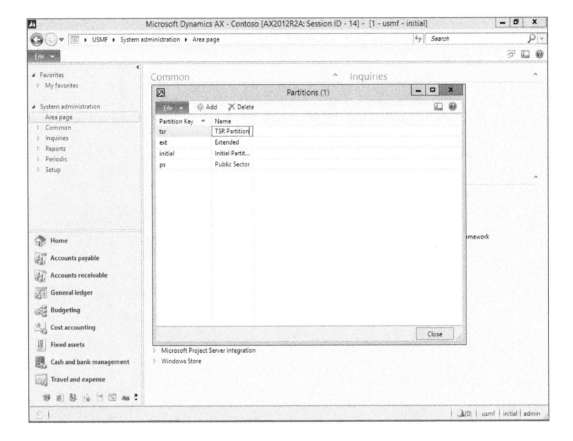

Then give your **Partition** record a **Primary Key** and also a **Name**.

When you have done that, click on the **Close** button to exit from the form.

Creating A New Shortcut To The Partition

After you have created a new **Partition** you need to create a shortcut that will allow you to open up an instance of Dynamics AX that points to it..

Creating A New Shortcut To The Partition

To do this, go to your desktop, and find an existing link to Dynamics AX.

Creating A New Shortcut To The Partition

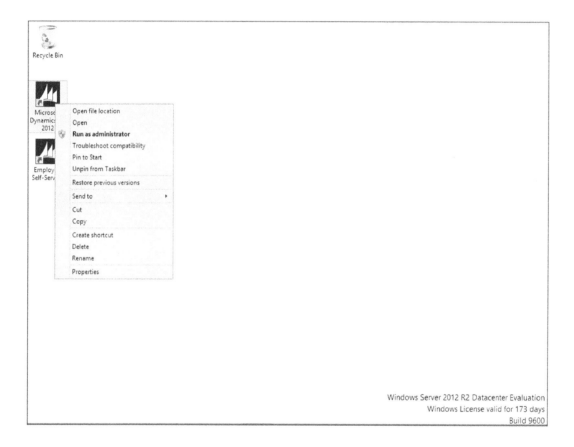

Right-mouse-click on the shortcut, and select the **Create Shortcut** option.

Creating A New Shortcut To The Partition

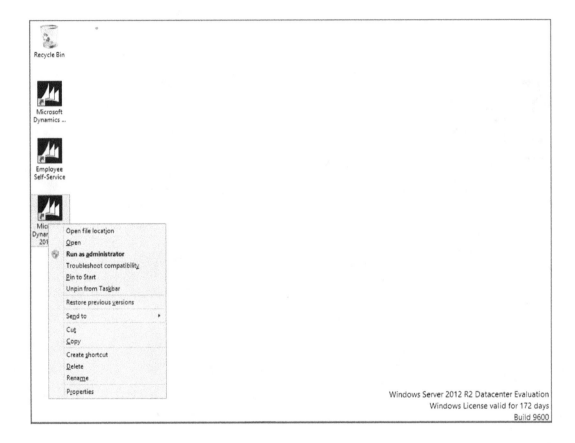

After the new shortcut has been created, right-mouse-click on the shortcut and select the **Properties** menu item.

Creating A New Shortcut To The Partition

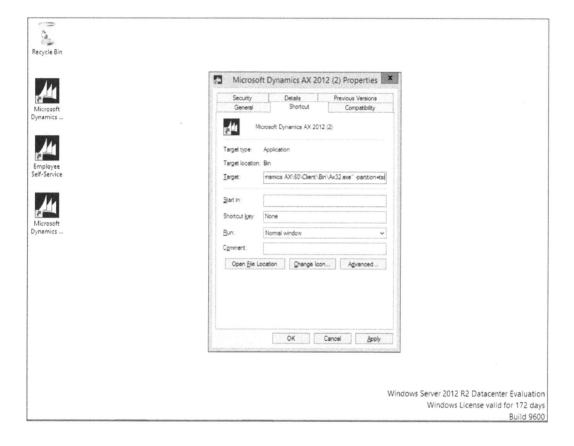

When the **Properties** dialog box is displayed, add the following text to the end of the **Target**:

-partition=*PartitionKey*

After you have done that you can close out of the shortcut properties.

Creating A New Shortcut To The Partition

All this is left to do is rename the shortcut so that you know this points to your new partition.

Initializing The Partition

Now that you can open up the **Partition** you can open it up and start setting it up. Dynamics AX will help you with this process as well by stepping you through an Initialization checklist.

Initializing The Partition

All you need to do to start the process is to double click on the new shortcut that you just created that points to your new partition.

Initializing The Partition

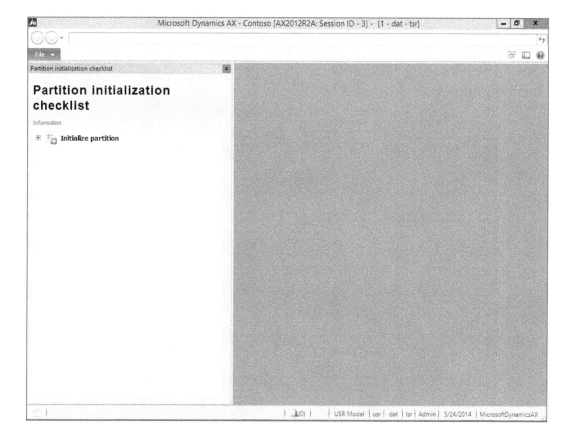

When Dynamics AX pops up it you will be taken into the **Partition Initialization Checklist.**

Initializing The Partition

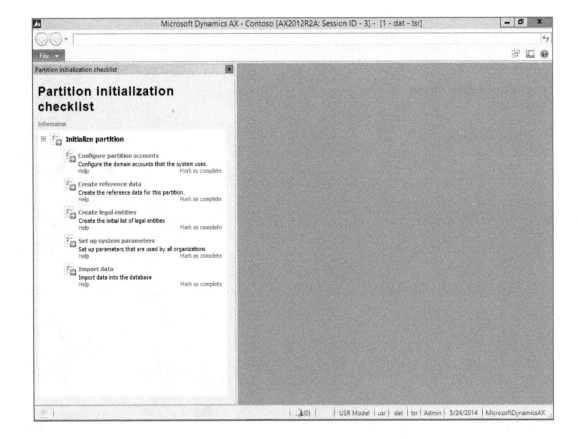

If you expand the checklist you will see all of the steps that you need to perform in order to set up your new system.

And the first step is to click on the **Configure Partition Accounts** link.

Initializing The Partition

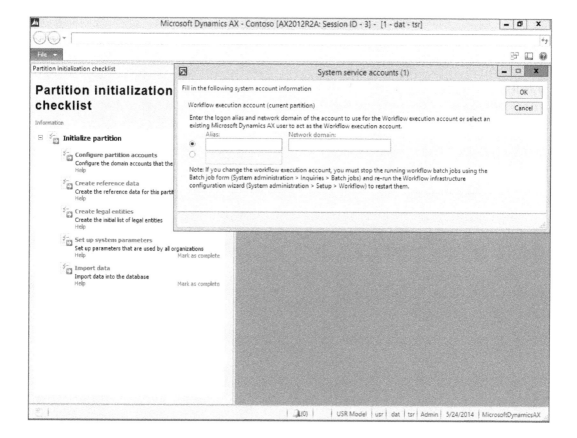

This will open up a dialog box asking you to define the **System Service Accounts**.

Initializing The Partition

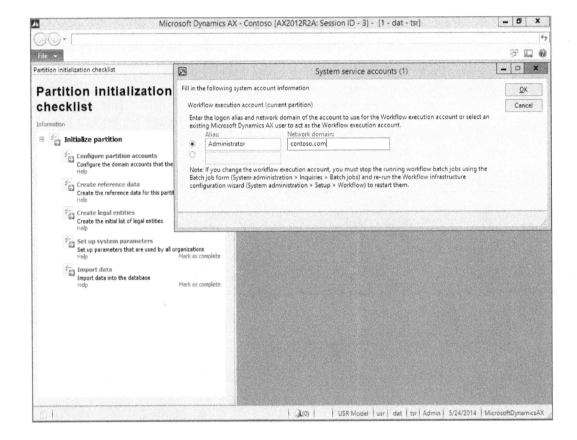

All you need to do is specify the **Alias** for the administrator user and also the **Network Domain**.

After you have done that, click on the **OK** button.

Initializing The Partition

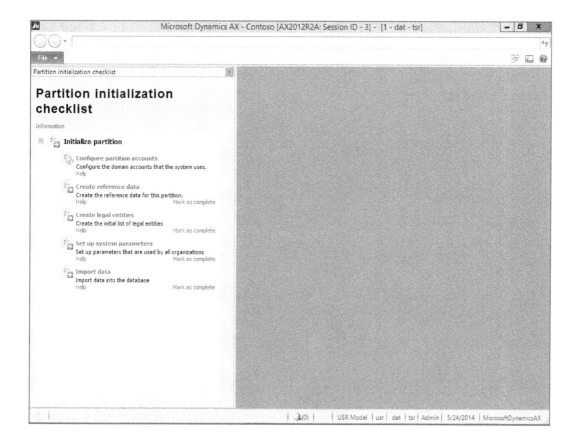

Now you will notice that the first step has been marked as completed. Now click on the **Create Reference Data** link.

Initializing The Partition

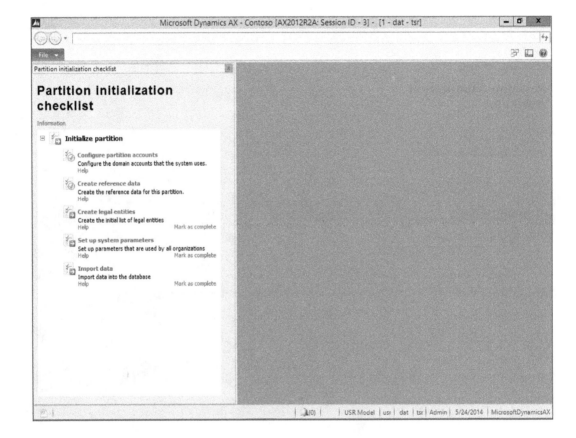

Dynamics AX will work for a couple of minutes and then the **Create Reference Data** step will mark itself as complete and you can then click on the **Create Legal Entities** step.

Initializing The Partition

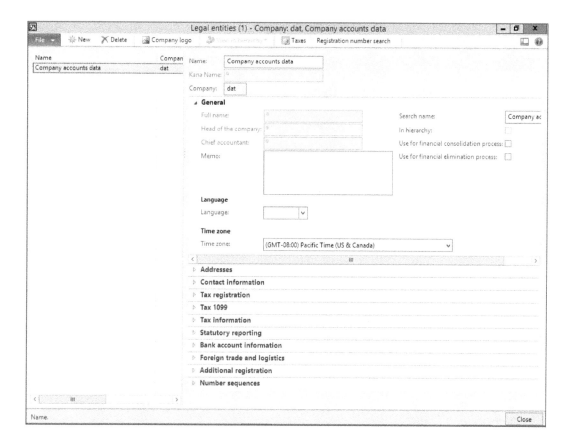

When the **Legal Entities** dialog box is displayed, click on the **New** button in the menu bar to create a new company.

Note: There will be a **dat** company already within your partition, but you don't want to use this as your main company – this is used to store reference data.

Initializing The Partition

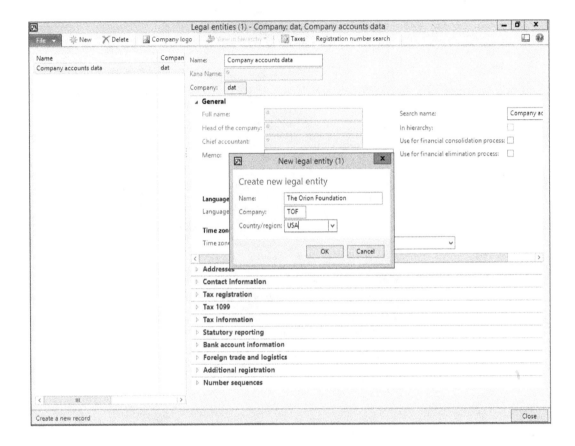

When the **New Legal Entity** dialog box is displayed, enter in a **Name**, a **Company** identifier, and also select your **Country/Region**.

When you have done that, just click on the **OK** button to exit from the form.

Initializing The Partition

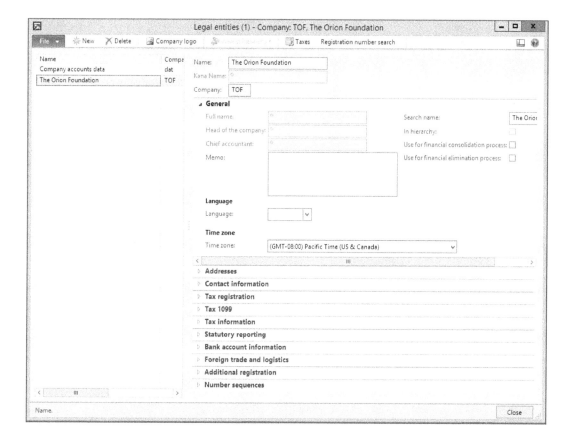

Now when you return to the **Legal Entities** you will see that you have a new entity to work with.

Initializing The Partition

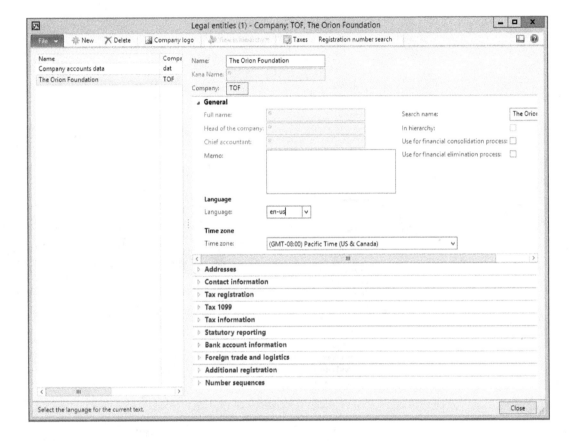

There are just a couple more things that you can do right now to tidy up the **Legan Entity**. The first one is to select a default **Language** for the entity.

Initializing The Partition

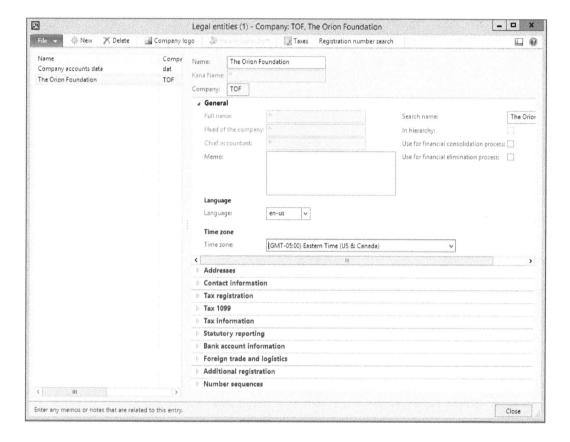

And the second is to specify the time zone (if you are not on Pacific time).

When you have done that, click on the **Close** button to exit from the form.

Initializing The Partition

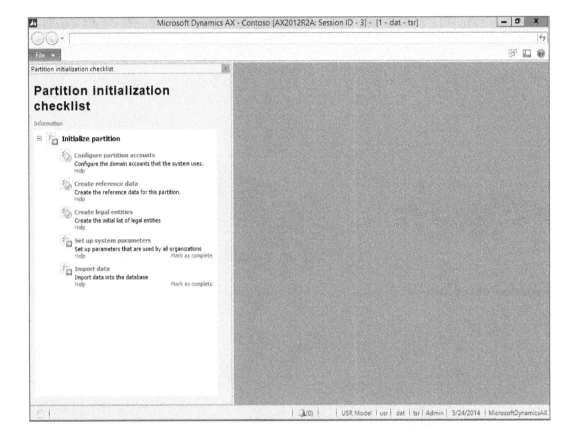

Now you will see that the checklist has moved you to the next step, so click on the **Setup System Parameters** link.

Initializing The Partition

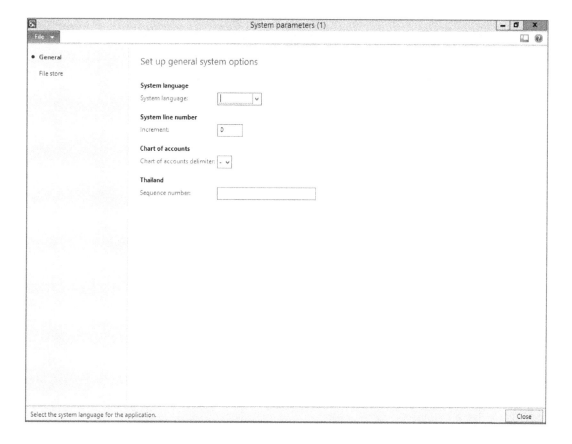

When the **System Parameters** maintenance form is displayed, start of by selecting the **General** page.

Initializing The Partition

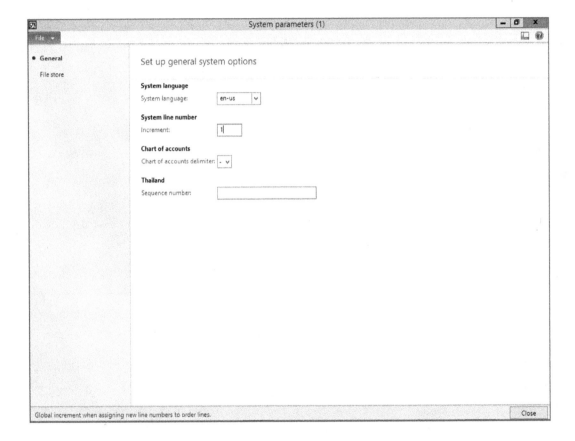

All you need to do here is specify the **System Language**, and also set the **Increment** value to 1.

Initializing The Partition

Then switch to the **File Store** page, and click on the folder icon to the right to the **Directory** field.

Initializing The Partition

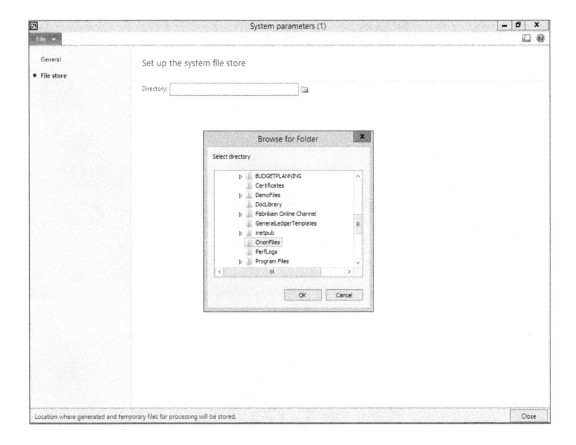

Navigate to the common location where you want all of the default files to be placed, and then click on the **OK** button.

Initializing The Partition

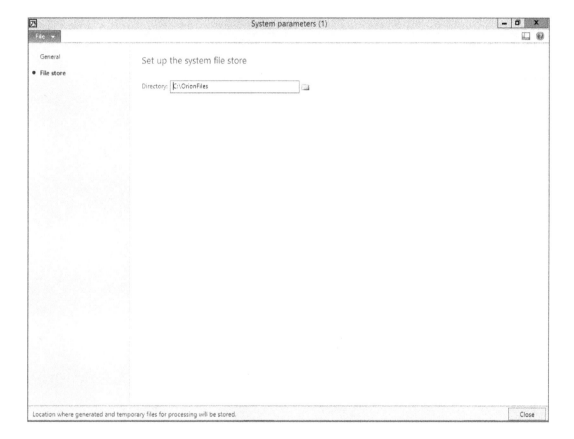

Once you have done that, just click on the **Close** button to exit from the form.

Initializing The Partition

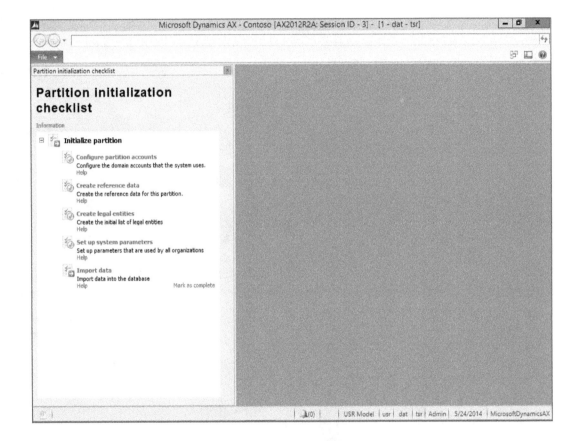

Now we have one step left. If you already have template data that you want to import into this legal entity, you can click on the **Import Data** link. But we don't have any at this point so we can skip this by clicking the **Mark As Complete** link.

Initializing The Partition

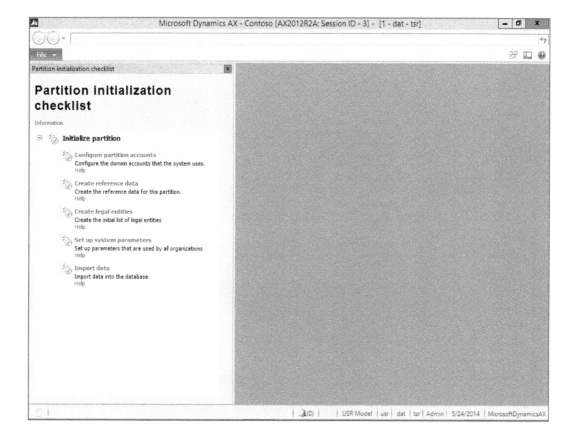

Now that everything has been completed, just close out of your Dynamics AX session and then re-open your partition.

Initializing The Partition

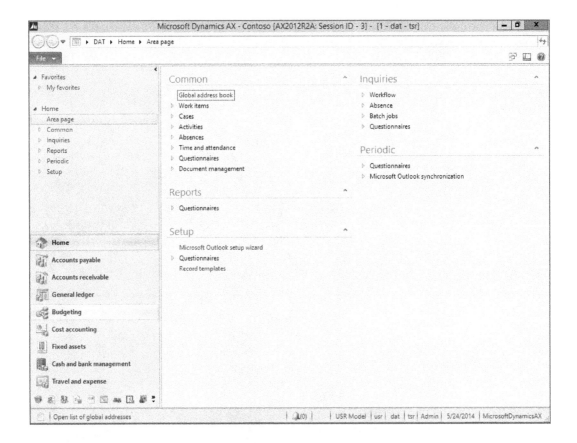

Now you will see something that look a lot more like what we want.

Initializing The Partition

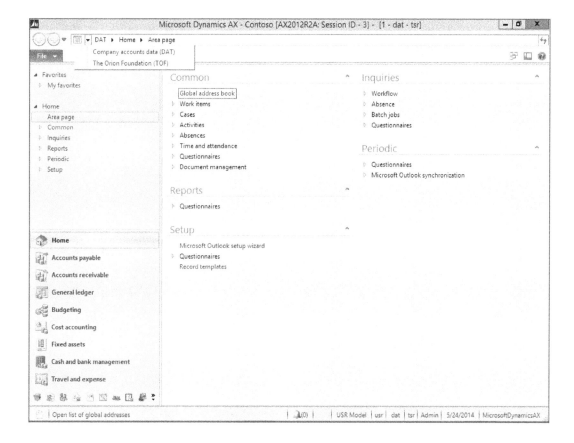

If you click on the first dropdown arrow of the breadcrumb bar, you will see that in addition to the **DAT** entity, you also have your new one that you just configured.

Initializing The Partition

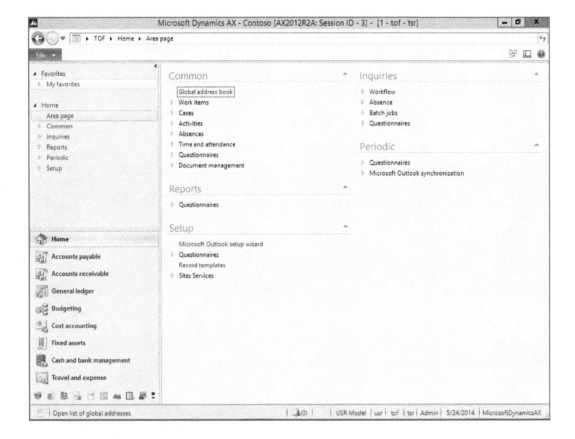

Now you can switch from the **DAT** company to your new one.

CONFIGURING THE SYSTEM FOR THE FIRST TIME

Once you have your new Partition set up, you will want to configure some of the system settings so that you get the best experience. This includes configuring some of the system parameters, configuring users, and also linking in some of the portals that you may want to take advantage of.

Changing The Default Company

You don't want to have to change your company from **DAT** every time you open up your partition, so it's a good idea at this point to change the default company that is associated with your user.

Changing The Default Company

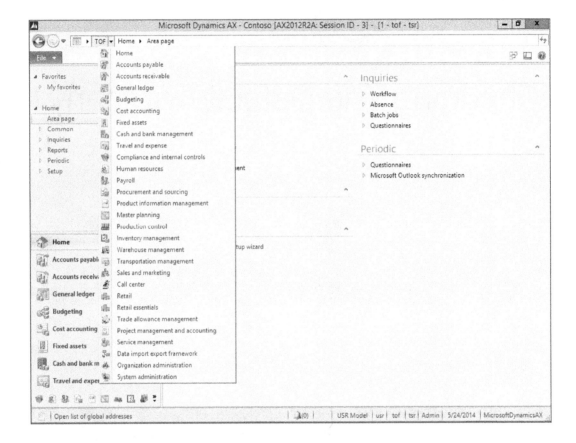

To do that, change to the **System Administration** area page wither through the navigation pad, or through the breadcrumb bar.

Changing The Default Company

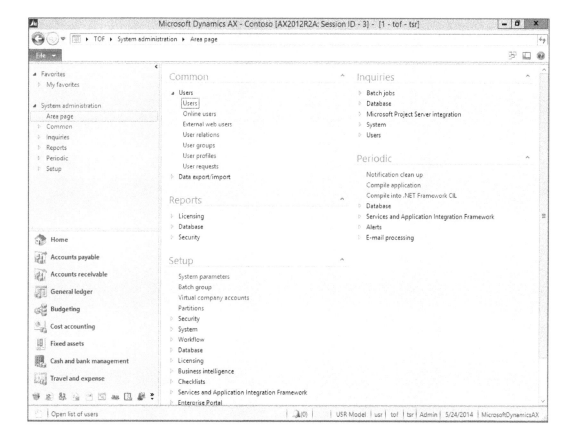

When the **System Administration** area page is displayed, click on the **Users** menu item within the **Users** folder of the **Common** group.

Changing The Default Company

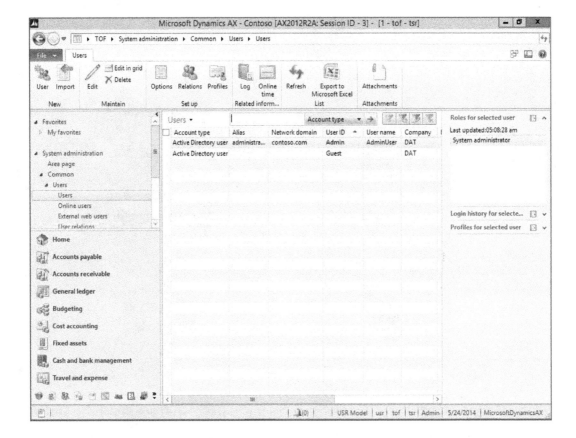

When the **Users** list page is displayed, you will notice that the default **Company** for your user is **DAT.** Double click on your user to open up the document view.

Changing The Default Company

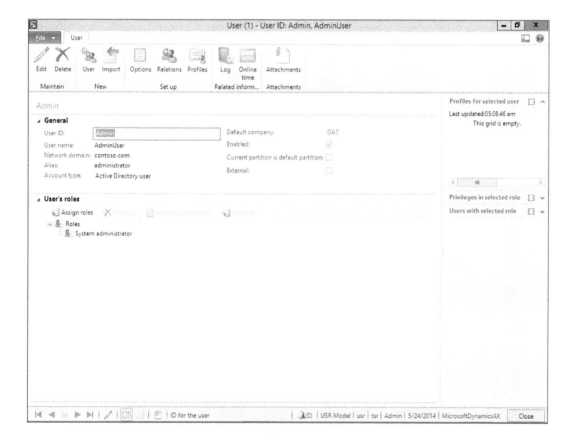

When the document view of the **User** is displayed, click on the **Edit** button within the **Maintain** group of the **User** action panel to change from display to edit mode.

Changing The Default Company

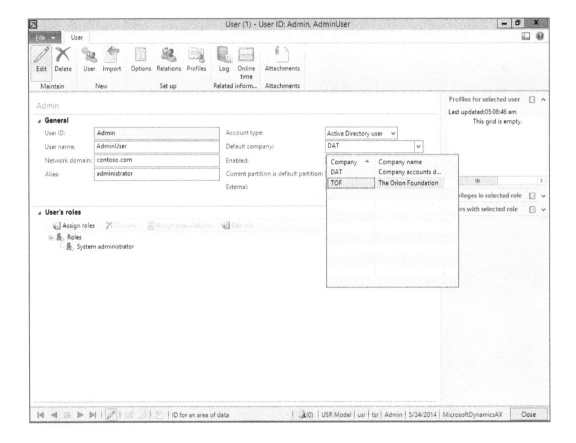

Now you will be able to change the **Default Company** for your user from **DAT** to your new company.

Changing The Default Company

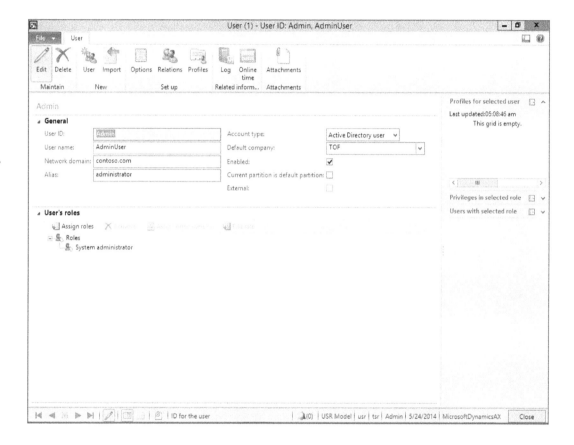

Once you have done that, just click on the **Close** button to exit from the form.

Changing The Default Company

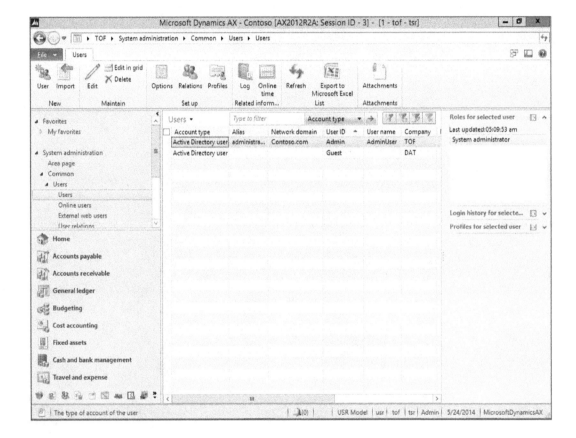

Now on the **Users** list page you will see that the user has a new Default **Company**.

Configure The Default Document Types Storage Locations

At this point, there is a little bit of housekeeping that you need to do in order to make your new partition purr. One of these is to configure your **Document Types** storage locations so that when you use your document attachments, Dynamics AX knows where to store them.

Configure The Default Document Types Storage Locations

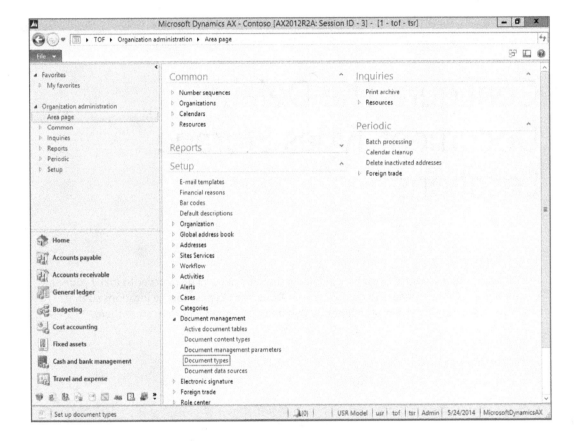

To do this, click on the **Document Types** menu item within the **Document Management** folder of the **Setup** group within the **System Administration** area page.

Configure The Default Document Types Storage Locations

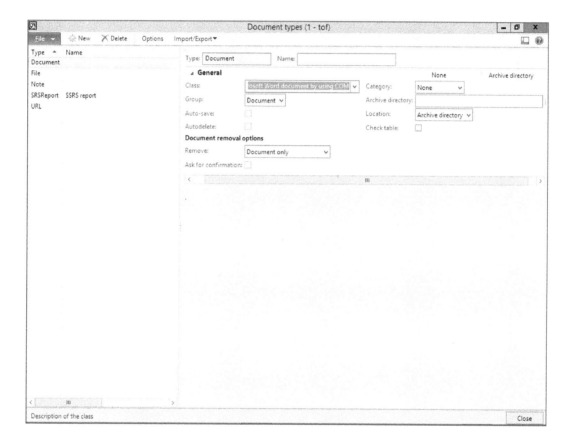

When the **Document Types** maintenance form is displayed you will see the default document types that have already been loaded into your partition. One problem though is that the document location is set to an **Archive Directory** but no **Archive Directory** has been specified.

Configure The Default Document Types Storage Locations

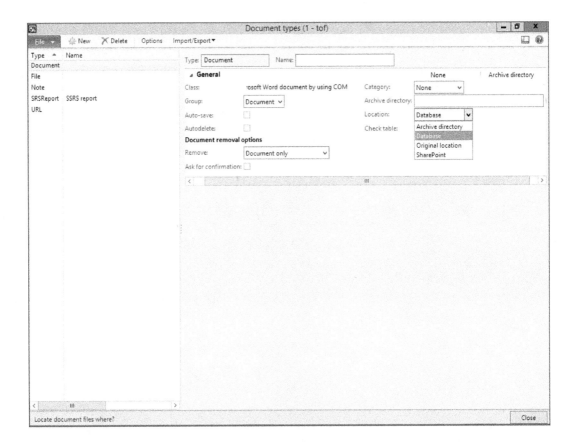

You can either specify a file path where you want to store the documents, or change the **Location** to **Database** to store them within the database itself.

Configure The Default Document Types Storage Locations

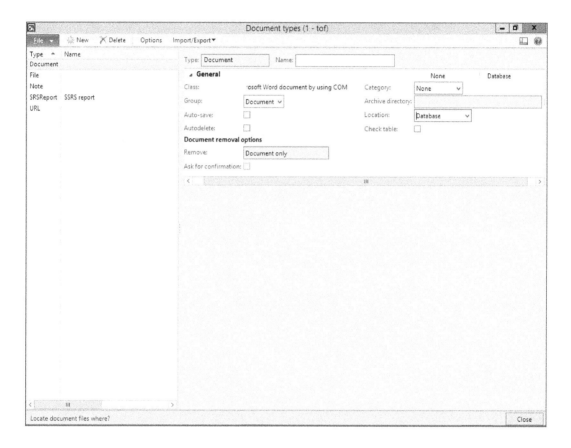

Once you do that the **Archive Directory** will become disabled and you are done.

Configure The Default Document Types Storage Locations

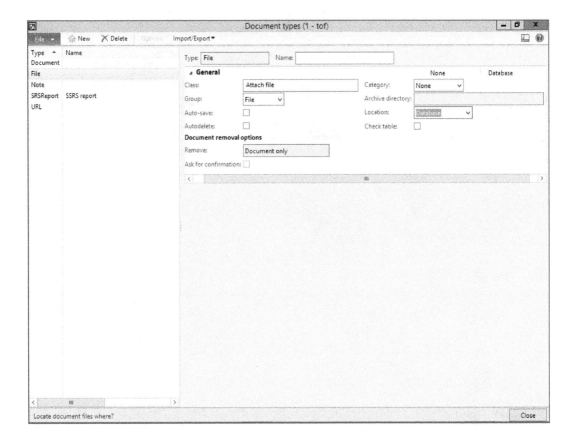

Look through all of the default **Document Types** and fix any other records. When you are done, click on the **Close** button to exit from the form.

Importing Default User Profiles

Now we will start configuring your users. Before we do that though we want to set up the **Default User Profiles** so that the users will be linked to role centers, and also have default privileges assigned to them. Luckily, we don't have to do this all by hand, Dynamics AX allows you to import all of these directly from its configuration database.

Importing Default User Profiles

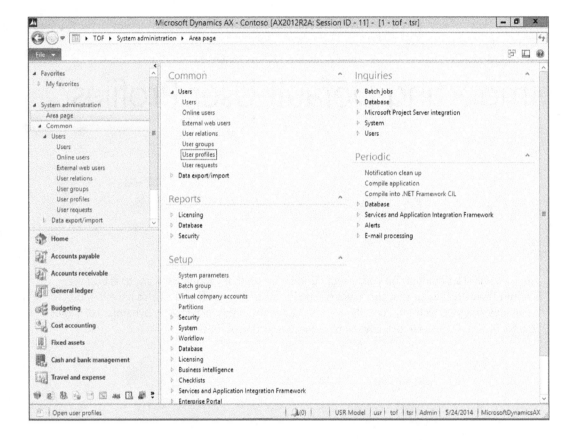

To do this, click on the **User Profiles** link within the **Users** folder of the **Common** group of the **System Administration** area page.

Importing Default User Profiles

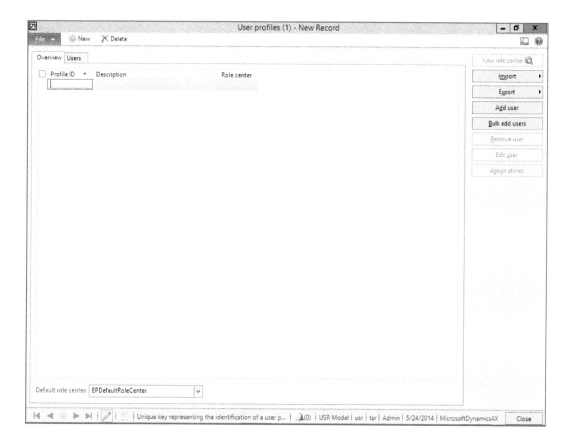

When the **User Profiles** list page is displayed, it will probably be completely empty.

Importing Default User Profiles

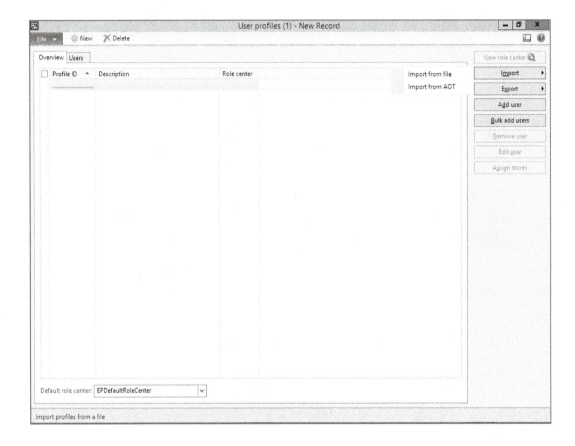

Click on the **Import** button to the right of the form, and select the **Import From AOT** menu item.

Importing Default User Profiles

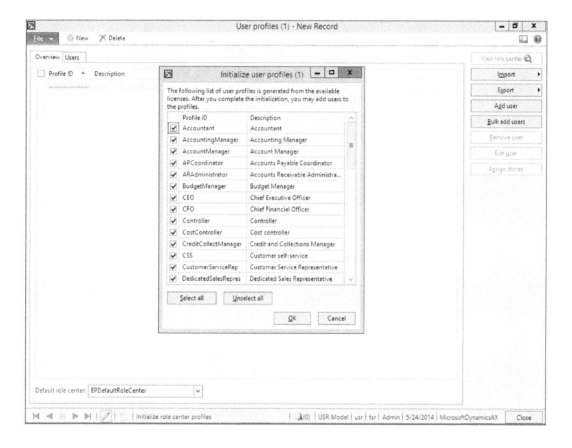

When the **Initialize User Profiles** dialog box is displayed, you will see all of the default user profiles within Dynamics AX. Click on the **Select All** button, and then click on the **OK** button.

Importing Default User Profiles

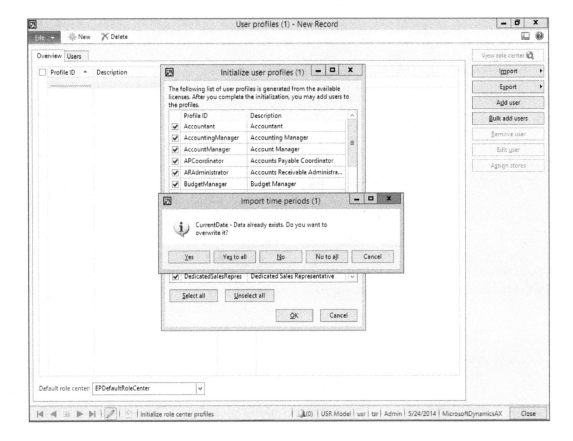

When the confirmation box is displayed, click on the **Yes To All** button.

Importing Default User Profiles

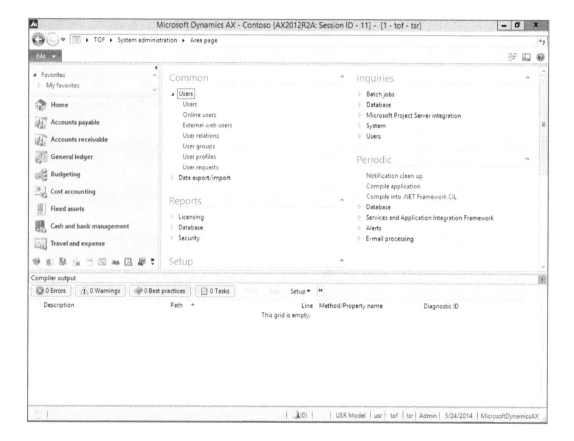

Since this is running a script in the background, the **Compiler Output** window may be displayed. If it does, then wait for it to complete, and then close the panel.

Importing Default User Profiles

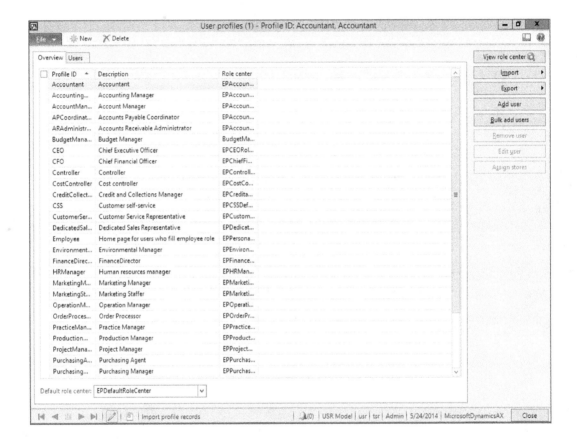

Now when you return to the **User Profiles** list page and refresh it (**F5**) you will see all of the default profiles have been loaded for you.

Adding Your User To A Role

Now that we have the default user profiles configured we can quickly add our user to the profile so that it is linked to a **Role Center**.

Adding Your User To A Role

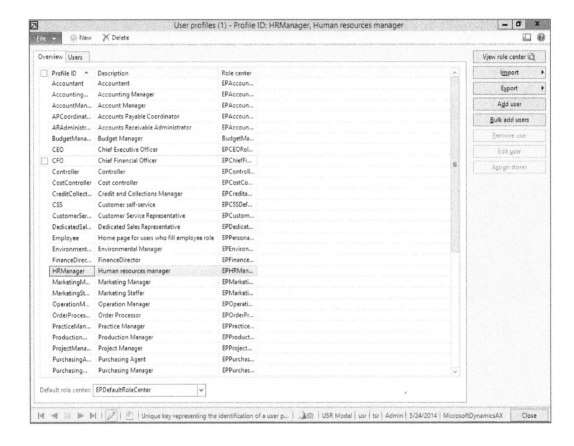

To do that, select the appropriate **Profile ID** for the administrator, and then click on the **Add User** button to the right of the form.

Adding Your User To A Role

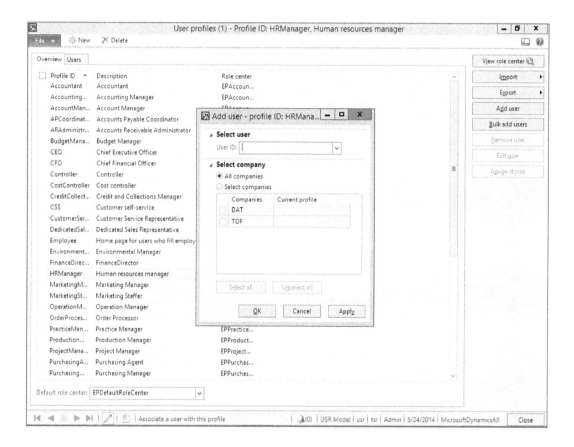

This will open up an **Add User** dialog box.

Adding Your User To A Role

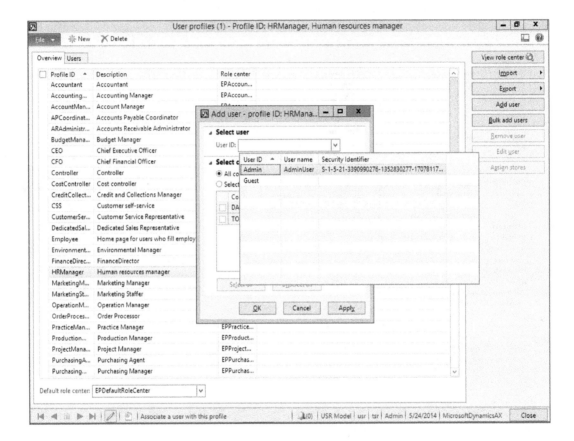

Select your user from the **User ID** dropdown box.

Adding Your User To A Role

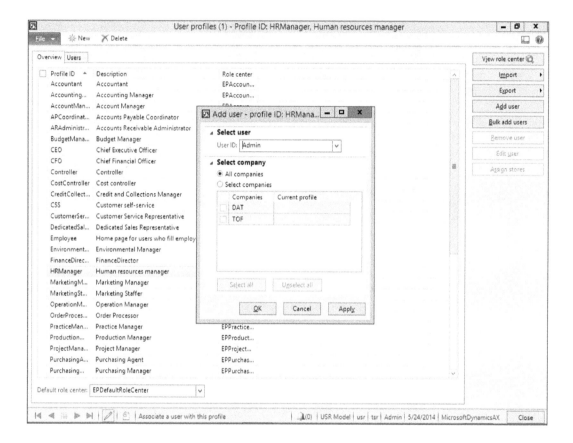

And then click on the **OK** button.

Adding Your User To A Role

If you switch to the **Users** tab for the **Profile ID** that you selected, you will now see that the user has been added to that profile.

Importing Additional Users

Right now you only have the administrator user configured within the Partition, so you will probably want to configure all of the other users that you want to have access to Dynamics AX. Luckily there is an import function that will allow you to grab all of the users directly from Active Directory, and load them in bulk which saves a lot of time and setup.

Importing Additional Users

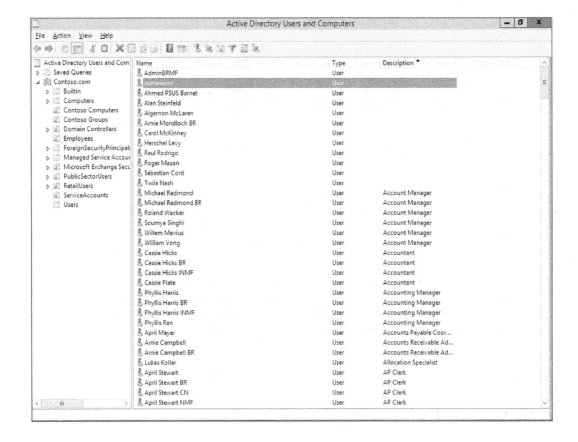

In my system I have a number of users already within Active Directory.

Importing Additional Users

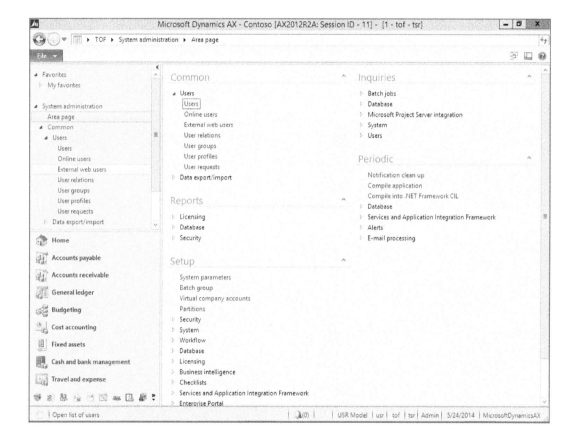

To import them in, click on the **Users** menu item within the **Users** folder of the **Common** group of the **System Administration** area page.

Importing Additional Users

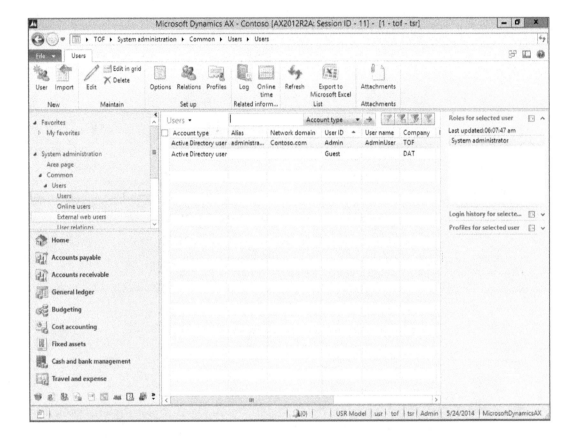

When the **Users** list page is displayed, click on the **Import** button within the **New** group of the **Users** action panel.

Importing Additional Users

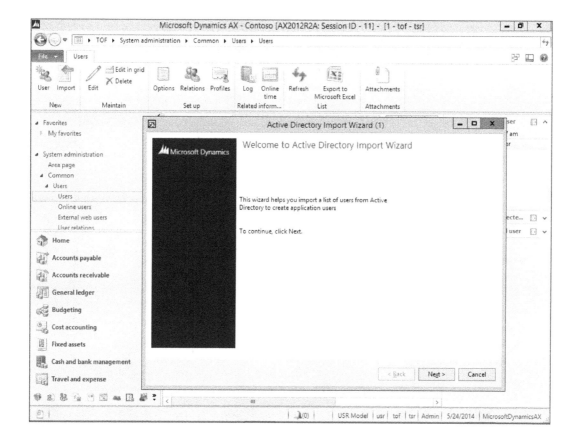

This will start off the import wizard. Just click **Next** to move on from the welcome page.

Importing Additional Users

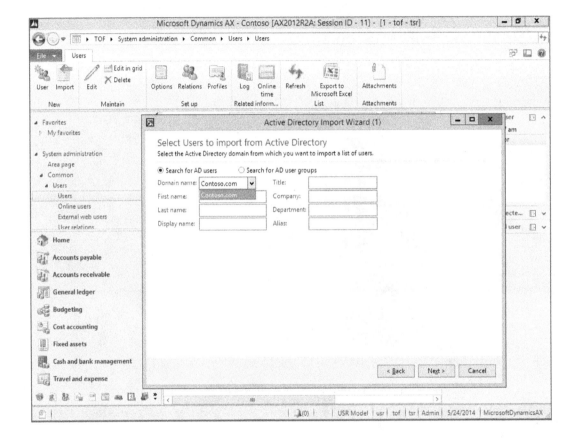

When on the **Select Users To Import from Active Directory** page, select the **Domain** that you want to search through for your users within Active Directory.

Importing Additional Users

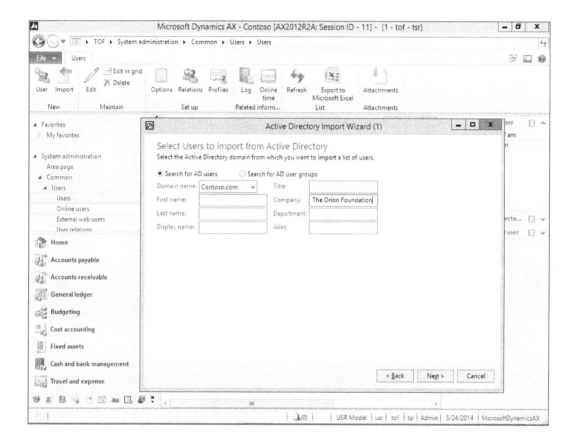

Then specify the search criteria that you want to use to filter out the users. In this case all of the users have the same **Company**.

Then click on the **Next** button.

Importing Additional Users

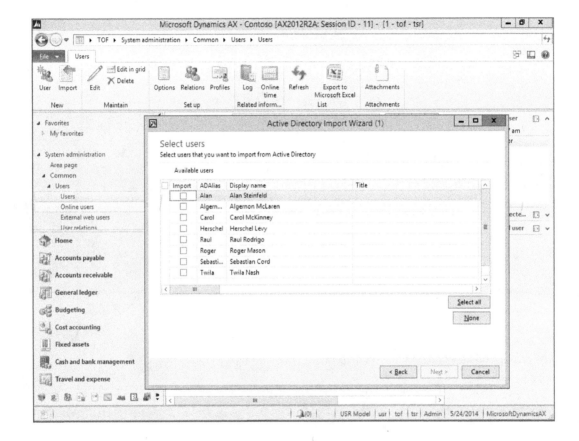

On the **Select Users** page you will see the users that matched your selection.

Importing Additional Users

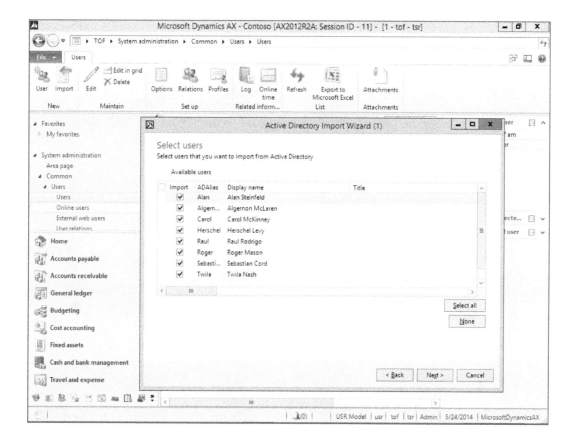

Click on the **Select All** button to select all of the users, or select the users that you want to import. Then click the **Next** button.

Importing Additional Users

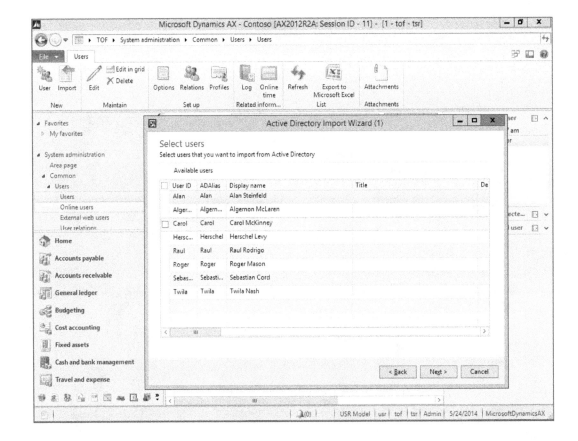

On the second **Select Users** page, just click on the **Next** button.

Importing Additional Users

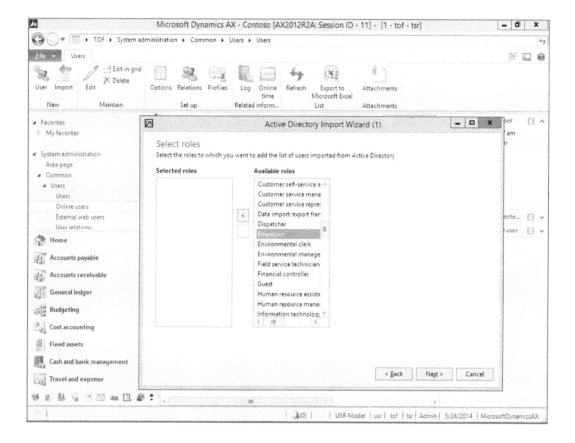

When the **Select Roles** page is displayed, select the default role that you want to assign to the users and then click on the < button.

Importing Additional Users

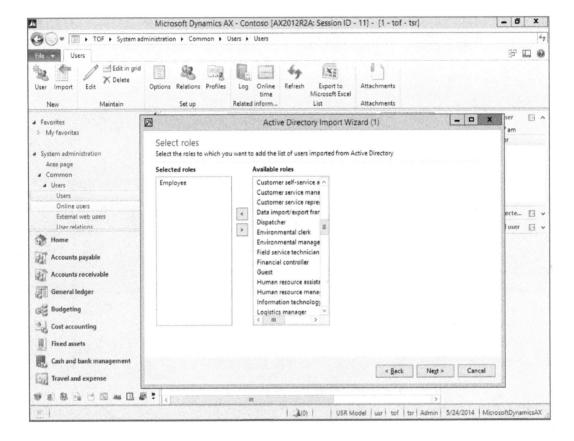

This will move the Role over into the **Selected Roles** panel and you can click the **Next** button to continue on.

Importing Additional Users

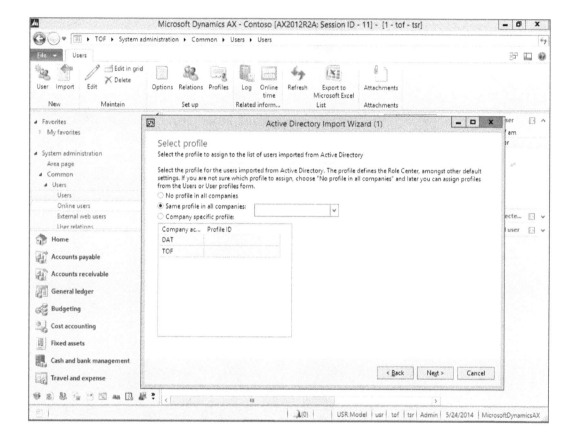

Finally when the **Select Profile** page is displayed you will need to select the default profile for the users.

Importing Additional Users

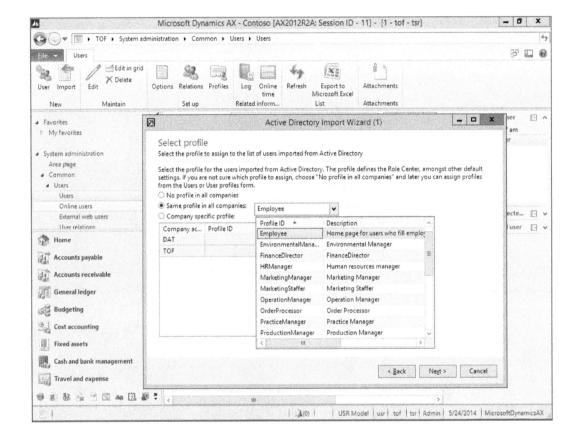

Click on the dropdown box for the **Same Profile In All Companies** field and select the profile that you want to assign to the users.

Importing Additional Users

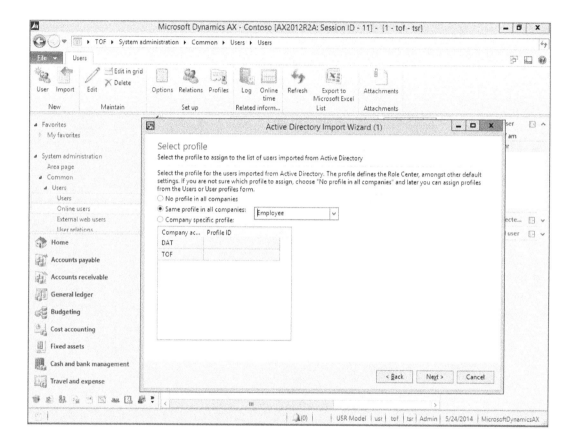

When you have done that, click on the **Next** button.

Importing Additional Users

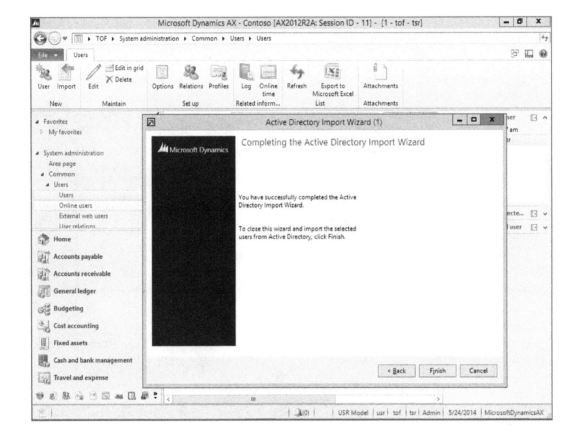

When the confirmation page is displayed, click on the **Finish** button.

Importing Additional Users

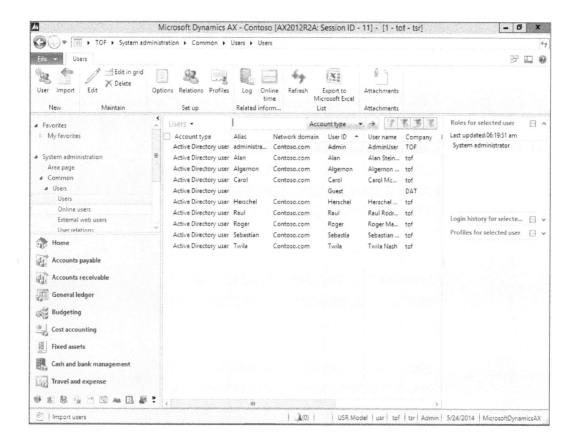

Now when you look at your **Users** list page you will see that all of your new users have been added to your system.

That was easy.

Configuring Enterprise Portal Links

Now that we have all of the users configured, we will probably want to take advantage of them by configuring the Enterprise Portal link so that we can then use the **Role Centers.**

Configuring Enterprise Portal Links

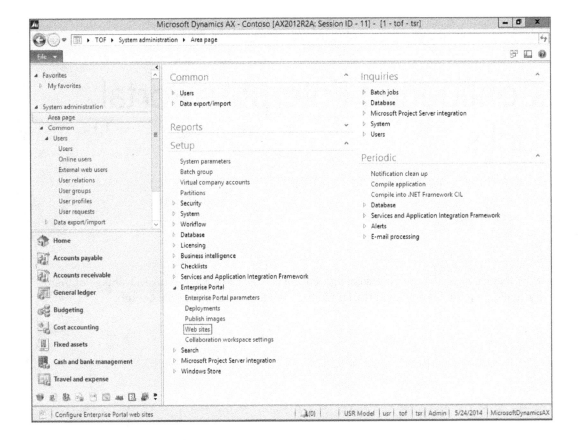

To do this, click on the **Web Sites** menu item within the **Enterprise Portal** folder of the **Setup** group within the **System Administration** area page.

Configuring Enterprise Portal Links

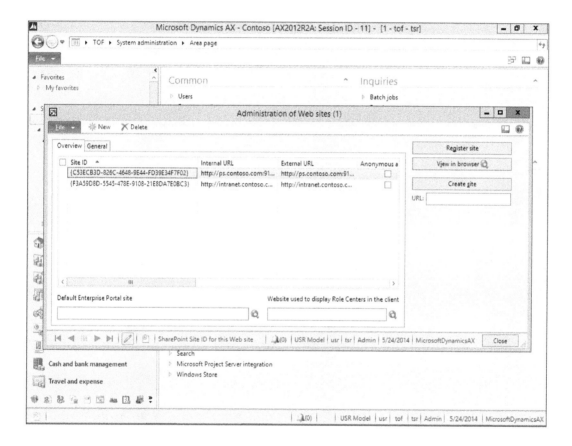

When the **Administration of the Web Sites** maintenance form is displayed, you will notice that the **Default Enterprise Portal** and **Website Used To Display Role Centers In The Client** links are empty.

Configuring Enterprise Portal Links

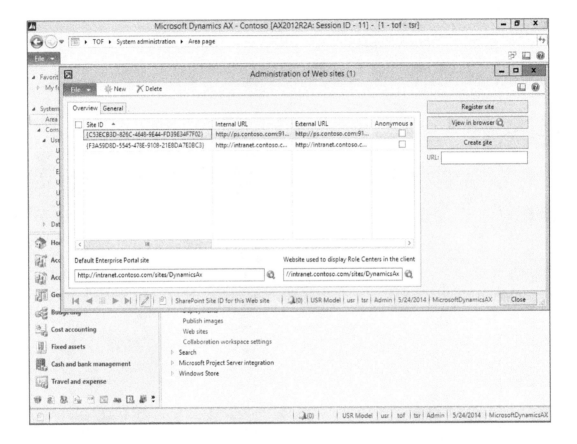

Just paste in the link to your Role Center base URL and then click the **Close** button.

Configuring Enterprise Portal Links

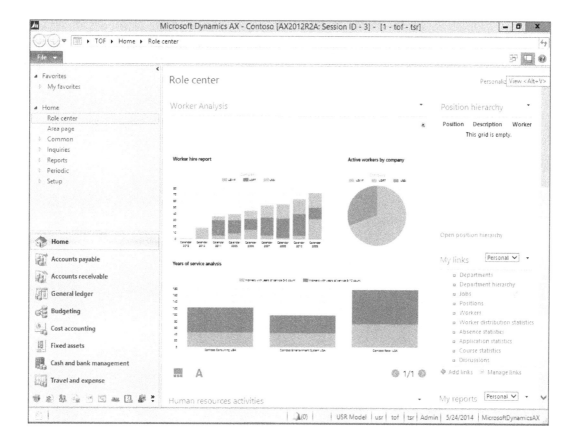

Now when you select the **Home** area page, a new option will be displayed that allows you to see the users **Role Center**.

That is too cool.

Configuring Enterprise Search Server

One final configuration tweak that we will make is to enable the **Search Server** within your new partition so that the users will be able to use it to find menu items and help more easily.

Configuring Enterprise Search Server

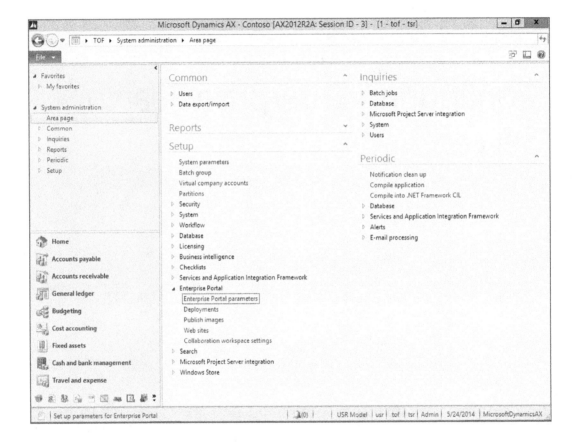

To do this, click on the **Enterprise Portal Parameters** link within the **Enterprise Portals** folder of the **Setup** group within the **System Administration** area page.

Configuring Enterprise Search Server

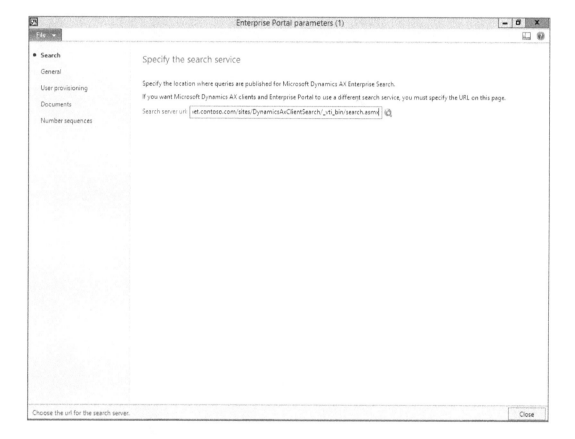

When the **Enterprise Portal Parameters** maintenance form is displayed, click on the **Search** page, and then paste in the URL for your **Search Service** that should have been installed with your base configuration. The default one is:

http://intranet.contoso.com/sites/DynamicsAxClientSearch/_vti_bin/search.asmx

Configuring Enterprise Search Server

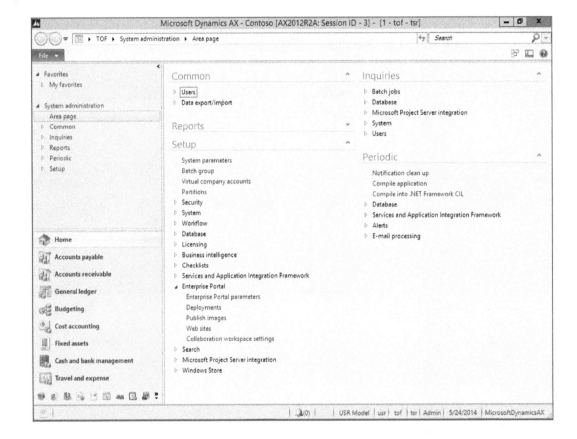

Now if you exit from your client and then re-open it, you will notice that there is a **Search** button in the top right of the form.

Configuring Enterprise Search Server

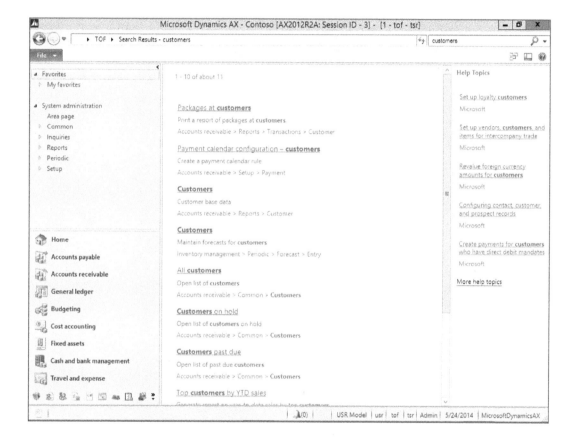

Just type in what you are looking for to test it out and you should get menu item links, data links, and also help links that relate to the search.

That will definitely be useful later on.

SUMMARY

Now you have the basic System configuration completed for Dynamics AX. All that is left for you to do is configure the application data.

About the Author

Murray Fife is a Microsoft Dynamics AX MVP, and Author with over 20 years of experience in the software industry.

Like most people in this industry he has paid his dues as a developer, an implementation consultant, a trainer, and now spend most of his days working with companies solving their problems with the Microsoft suite of products, specializing in the Dynamics® AX solutions.

EMAIL	murray@murrayfife.me
TWITTER	@murrayfife
SKYPE	murrayfife
AMAZON	http://www.amazon.com/author/murrayfife
BLOG	http://dynamicsaxtipoftheday.com
	http://extendingdynamicsax.com
	http://atinkerersnotebook.com
SLIDESHARE	http://slideshare.net/murrayfife
LINKEDIN	http://www.linkedin.com/in/murrayfife

www.ingramcontent.com/pod-product-compliance
Lightning Source LLC
Chambersburg PA
CBHW080419060326
40689CB00019B/4306